Original title:

Meaning in Life (and Other Things You Forget)

Author: Miriam Kensington

ISBN HARDBACK: 978-1-80566-141-2

ISBN PAPERBACK: 978-1-80566-436-9

Silence as a Forgotten Companion

In the midst of a noisy crowd,
My thoughts like stray cats meowed.
Searching for wisdom in every shout,
Only to find my mind in doubt.

I asked a goldfish for advice,
It just swam in circles, oh so nice.
A wise old turtle shrugged the fuss,
Said, "Don't rush, life's a big bus!"

Pigeons cooed, offering their two cents,
But their logic made no real sense.
I pondered with coffee and cakes,
Did they forget their own mistakes?

I sought solace in the stillness,
Where absurd meets the thrill of illness.
What's life without a wink and grin?
At least my puns had a good spin!

A Tapestry Woven with Shadows

In shadows played the jokes of old,
Laughter weaves a tale so bold.
Knitted thoughts in colors bright,
Stitched together, day and night.

But tangled threads all lose their way,
A sock lost in the grand ballet.
When life's a quilt of mishmash smiles,
And missing pieces stretch for miles.

Reflection in a Broken Mirror

A shard reflects my lopsided grin,
As logic plays a trick again.
Each crack a tale, a giggle shared,
In my own funhouse, I'm unprepared.

Winks at me from edges rough,
Telling me that I'm more than fluff.
Through every flaw, my smile beams,
Oh, life's a patchwork of wild dreams!

Dandelion Wishes in the Wind

Blow the fluff, make a grand wish,
Reality laughs, that's the dish!
Each puff a chuckle in disguise,
Floating hopes in the sunny skies.

Grab a weed, dance with the breeze,
Nature giggles, oh how it teases!
What's success, if not a joke,
Just far-off dreams and dandelion smoke?

Conversations with a Fading Star

I chat with stars, they're quite aloof,
Sharing tales from way up there, proof!
A twinkle here, a wisp of light,
Time has a sense of humor, right?

They giggle back, "What's time to us?"
"Find joy, my friend, in all the fuss!"
Cosmic whispers full of glee,
Life's a jest, let it be free!

Fleeting Echoes

I missed my train, it left at noon,
But here I am, still in my room.
I ponder deep, like a wise old sage,
But forgot my lines, now I'm on stage.

Life's a dance, I often trip,
My coffee spills, oh what a drip!
The joy's in chaos, that's the catch,
But where's my bag? Ah, what a scratch!

The Weight of Forgotten Dreams

I once had plans to scale a peak,
Now I binge on shows for a week.
With snacks as my trusty sidekick friend,
Who needs a goal when Doritos blend?

I penned a book, it got one line,
"A tale so grand, it simply shines!"
But life just laughed, threw it in the bin,
Now I write poetry on a whim.

Whispers in the Dust

I clean my house, dust on the floor,
Then lose the broom—what's it for?
The cat just stares, unimpressed,
While I chase my thoughts like a restless pest.

With a million dreams under a bed,
Why's the laundry piled up instead?
I gaze at stars, and then I yawn,
Tomorrow's list? It's already gone.

Shadows of Yesterday

I sat and pondered life's great quest,
But really thought about my rest.
The sun was bright, the day was long,
Yet here I am with just one song.

I asked a sage about my fate,
He laughed so hard, it felt like fate!
He said, "Why worry? Just take a nap!"
And that's the wisdom — oh, what a trap!

A Symphony of Unanswered Questions

Why's the sky so far away,
Yet my socks are lost today?
Do birds ever get lost too,
Or just fly north for a brew?

What if cats had secret shops,
With tuna treats and fancy props?
Can plants hear you when you sing,
Or just judge you for the bling?

Is my chair aware of my plight,
As I ponder things at night?
Do shadows long for the sun's glow,
Or just chill out and take it slow?

Oh the woes of thought's parade,
With questions that lead to charade.
I guess I'll just keep on asking,
While life's sweet moments are basking.

The Pathways We Overlook

Once I took a left instead,
Found a frog wearing a fed.
He croaked out life's best advice,
'Just hop along, it's quite nice!'

Stumbled on a garden gnome,
Claimed he wished to leave his home.
Said he'd like to travel far,
Instead he's stuck with that jar.

Sidewalk cracks, the neighborhood chat,
Discussing if squirrels wear a hat.
They scurry with their tiny schemes,
While I just chase outlandish dreams.

So let's take the roads less traveled,
Where all the curious things unraveled.
We'll laugh at paths we never tread,
With stories of the gnome instead.

Fleeting Moments, Lasting Imprints

Here's to coffee that's grown cold,
With tales of laughter, dreams untold.
The puppy sleeps in a sunbeam,
While I chase after life's wild dream.

Did I leave the oven on today?
Or is it just my mind at play?
The toast burned crisp, a little black,
But that's the meal I won't look back.

Moments pass like quicksand grains,
Yet I still ponder little pains.
Did I eat the cake or just the crumbs?
Counting calories, here it comes!

Glances shared on crowded streets,
With strangers who remain discreet.
In the chaos, we find our spot,
In fleeting moments, joy's what we've got.

The Dance of Forgotten Memories

Remember when I slipped on ice?
And made a snow angel, oh so nice?
That epic fall that brightened my day,
Now it's a tale that never fades away.

Prom night hair and glittered shoes,
Why do we always have the blues?
A dance with friends, embarrassing moves,
Yet somehow we all find our grooves.

Crisp autumn leaves and high school dreams,
Chasing laughter like rippling streams.
With every stumble, every misstep,
Life's a dance, it's all one big pep!

So let's waltz through this jumbled goo,
With memories woven, they stick like glue.
We may forget, but joy will persist,
In the dance of life, we can't resist.

A Library of Lost Hopes

In a shelf of dusty dreams,
We find the things we seek.
The bookmarks of forgotten schemes,
All stacked up, unique.

Coffee stains where poems ran,
And memos left unread.
A puzzled look where wisdom can,
Be found beneath the spread.

Between the tomes our laughter grows,
Like moths caught in a flame.
We trip on words, but who still knows,
The source of our acclaim?

So grab a book and take a chance,
Forget what books have said.
In this library's merry dance,
We laugh while feeling spread.

The Sunlight Between the Cracks

In tiny beams where shadows meet,
A warm glow starts to play.
We trip on light with clumsy feet,
And giggle through the day.

Pavement cracks the perfect stage,
For sunlight's daring acts.
The curtains twitch, just like a page,
With meanings in the facts.

A dance of clouds, a sprightly breeze,
As we forget to care.
In daylight's glow, we feel the tease,
And laughter fills the air.

So if you seek what's felt profound,
Just look where laughs are found.
For in those rays between the cracks,
The joy of life abounds.

Fleeting Glimpses of Eternity

In sneezes and in hiccup fits,
The cosmos gives a nod.
A dance of moments, tiny bits,
That leave us feeling fraud.

With every glance we steal a spark,
A chuckle from the stars.
Each giggle echoes in the dark,
Turning light from our scars.

Like ice cream melting in the sun,
We chase the dripping cheer.
In fleeting sips, our races run,
Unraveling our fear.

So take a breath and please don't rush,
These moments wink and play.
In laughter's soft, embracing hush,
We find our vibrant way.

Silent Lullabies of Existence

Beneath the surface, whispers churn,
Of dreams that float like dust.
In quiet tones, we twist and turn,
In laughter's gentle trust.

With pillows made of chuckled sighs,
We rest our weary heads.
In midnight chuckles, cosmic ties,
Are woven in our beds.

From bedtime stories turned to jest,
These lullabies do play.
We find the humor in the quest,
As life slips by our way.

So hold your heart and hear the tune,
As silence starts to dance.
For in the giggles of the moon,
We find our sweet romance.

Fables of the Unlived Years

In the closet sit old shoes,
Once meant for a grand debut.
They giggle as they gather dust,
Time's trickster, always makes us bust.

A half-eaten cake sits on the shelf,
It mocks my desire to be someone else.
With bites that echo what could've been,
Like dreams I forgot but now see again.

The cat's in charge, it's plain to see,
While I'm here scrolling endlessly.
She yawns as I chase wild plans,
Life's comedy, oh how it spans.

Each moment slips like soap in hand,
I joke with fate, a fickle band.
With laughter loud, I find my ground,
In fables lost, my joys are found.

Reveries of a Soul's Journey

A sock goes missing, where's it fled?
To realms unknown, or under the bed?
I search and sigh, with high hopes pinned,
That each lost thing is where it should've been.

I dream of sailing on a spaghetti sea,
With meatball islands just for me.
But wake in bed, what a shame!
I guess my fish has lost its name.

The toaster's stuck in morning's trance,
While my coffee cup does little dance.
In this kitchen, life's laughter brews,
Witty monologues and gentle hues.

I wander paths of silly thought,
Laughing at battles I never fought.
In reveries, I stroll with glee,
Finding joy in the absurdity.

The Pendulum of What Remains

A clock ticks loud, its dance is sly,
It tells me time but makes me sigh.
With every chime, a thought is lost,
Like ice cream drips, just at a cost.

Socks that don't match, oh what a sight,
A fashion statement in the wrong light.
I wear them proud, defying trends,
What fun it is, laughing with friends.

The fridge hums tunes of days gone by,
Pickles and jams whispering why.
In every jar, a story hides,
Of meals and tales, and bouncy rides.

From childhood dreams to midnight snacks,
The pendulum swings, no looking back.
So I dance to life's delightful song,
In absurdity, we all belong.

Beneath the Weight of Yesterdays

Buried under stacks of old regrets,
Lies a pizza box, its fate foretells.
A slice untouched, a relic of time,
Each bite I didn't take feels like a crime.

My phone pings loud with memes and dreams,
The wisdom shared, or so it seems.
In chats we giggle, life on a loop,
As if the mundane is some cosmic scoop.

With socks on heels, I traipse along,
Singing off-key, but hey, it's a song!
Each note I miss, each laugh I snort,
Are badges earned in this absurd sport.

Beneath these layers of yesterday's haze,
I find my chuckles in remarkable ways.
For every slip and miss on the way,
Lies laughter's light, brightening my play.

Fleeting Moments on Worn Out Paths

One sock's gone missing in the wash,
It dances like a rogue, what a posh!
Lost in the lint of fleeting days,
I chase it down in laughter's haze.

The coffee spills upon my shirt,
A masterpiece of caffeine dirt.
Waved at the neighbor with a grin,
Only to realize, I forgot my chin.

My pet goldfish gives me the stare,
With bubbles poppin' and nary a care.
I ponder life, oh where should I dwell?
The fish just swims, it's doing swell.

A cactus sits upon my desk,
Its prickly ways are quite grotesque.
Yet somehow in its thorny flair,
I find a joy in living rare.

Beneath the Surface of Routine

The toaster pops, I jump in fright,
It's morning madness, not a delight.
Toast lands butter-side down once more,
A crispy fate that I abhor.

The cat meows, demands a snack,
She struts around, with perfect smack.
I wonder if life's just cat and crumbs,
With purrs that echo and silly hums.

I searched for my keys beneath the couch,
Found a dust bunny that made me crouch.
Each day's a puzzle without the clues,
Or maybe I'm just terrible with shoes.

The plants in corners complain and sigh,
They thrive on neglect as days go by.
With all their green in silent chat,
It's good to know it's fine to chat.

The Dance of Forgotten Echoes

A shoe on the left, another on the right,
They tango around in morning light.
With mismatched pairs, I step out bold,
The street's my stage, let stories unfold.

My phone buzzes, a random thought,
Reminding me of all that I've fought.
Yet here I stand, just lost in space,
Is it a battle or just a race?

I trip on echoes of laughter past,
Moments that linger, surprisingly fast.
Like bubble gum stuck to my shoe,
Some memories taste sweet, some leave a bruise.

In a world of alerts, I sometimes forget,
What really sparks joy or acts as a net.
Yet here I stand, just humming a tune,
And maybe that's the best thing to do soon.

In the Cradle of Silent Questions

Why does the fridge hum a sad song?
As if it's tired of where it belongs.
With leftovers who play hide and seek,
I ponder life while I take a peek.

Each night's a riddle I can't decode,
Like socks in the dryer, they roam the road.
With questions that dangle, I sip some tea,
The answer's a party where I'm not free.

The plants whisper tales of old,
Of things that matter and treasures untold.
I nod and pretend to understand,
While plotting my escape to a distant land.

A tinkle of spoons, a dish that breaks,
Life's rhythm sways with tiny mistakes.
Yet in the chaos, I find a spark,
Waking up slowly beneath the dark.

Threads of Invisible Purpose

In the laundry basket, socks do hide,
Each one a story, worn with pride.
But find a match? It's an endless spree,
Dancing alone, just like me.

The cat in the sun, he stretches wide,
Planning world domination as he glides.
But a fly buzzes by, and off he goes,
Purpose forgotten, chasing shadows.

Grandpa talks of riches, once far and bright,
While I daydream of pizza, late at night.
Is cash truly king? Or do we all seek,
The smallest of pleasures, the joy of the week?

So here's to the quests, both grand and small,
To finding our socks, or answering a call.
In the dance of the mundane, don't lose your beat,
There's hilarity found in life's little cheat.

In Search of Lost Lighthouses

A sailor once sailed where the fog rolled thick,
Searching for beacons, oh what a trick!
But ships found the shore by not looking back,
His compass a guppy, lost in the snack.

They said, 'Here's the map,' but it pointed wrong,
To where jellyfish danced and the oysters sung.
He built a lighthouse from pies and bread,
A beacon for seagulls; they shrugged instead.

A crab waved its claws, wanting some fun,
While dolphins and pelicans basked in the sun.
Forget the grand lights, the fanciful charts,
Sometimes the laughter is where adventure starts.

So raise your glass high—here's to the lost!
They guide us with whimsy, despite the cost.
In pursuit of the beams, in oceans untamed,
You'll find that the journey is what can't be named.

Canvas of Unwritten Poems

A blank page whispers, 'Come play with me!'
But my pen sits quietly, sipping green tea.
What if I name this a magnum opus?
Or doodle a fish, call it joyous?

Words tumble like kittens, chasing their tails,
While thoughts lean on clouds with highly-strung sails.
Is that a metaphor for missing a line?
Or just dinner's promise of not-so-fine wine?

A sonnet of coffee stains and toast,
Why write about life when I can make the most?
Cup half full, half empty, it starts to bleed,
Hey! That's my heart! Should've planted a seed!

So here's to the canvas with patches of fate,
Where ink spills like laughter, both silly and great.
We'll scribble our stories, or leave them to fate,
In the scrapbook of nonsense, let's celebrate!

Remnants of a Distant Star

In the sky's vastness, a twinkle says, 'Hi!'
Echoes of thoughts that drift and pry.
But hold on tight, they may float away,
Just like my diet when cookies do play.

A comet speeds past, with a tail full of wish,
While I'm here wondering what's for my dish.
Do stars write themselves, in cosmic delight?
Or do they fumble too, in the depths of the night?

Wish upon a sparkle, then laugh at the try,
For dreams are intentions that wobble and fly.
But hold onto joy, it's a glimmering spark,
Like trying to hang onto a dog in the park!

So here's to the remnants of far-off bright flames,
That nudge us to chuckle and play silly games.
In the vast night of nonsense, let's share our quirks,
For the best bits of stardust are found in our quirks.

A Whisper from the Abyss

In the depths of a sock drawer, so sly,
Lies treasure chests of lint, oh my!
Lost memories of keys, that turned the lock,
Twist your fate, like a wobbly clock.

Pondering pizza toppings in dreams,
Life's secret is buried in cheese-filled seams.
Will I ever resolve my taco debates?
In this grand maze, what truly awaits?

Hitchhiking through thoughts, a bus with no brakes,
Sipping on milkshakes, watching life flake.
The universe giggles, its whims take their toll,
Almonds can't dance, but they sure play a role.

So let's toast to forgetfulness, cheers with a grin,
For what we forget helps us begin.
Life's a jigsaw, pieces askew,
Hey! What was I saying? Oh well, adieu!

Portraits of Forgotten Journeys

There's a map on the wall, but it's lost its way,
Where the X marks the spot? No one can say.
Follow the doodles, they might lead you right,
To a treasure of snacks on a lazy night.

The cat on the couch wears a crown of fluff,
And claims he's wise, though he's had quite enough.
Points of interest marked by crumbs and hair,
In the kingdom of lazies, do we even care?

The only direction is inventing your song,
Who knew that wrong turns could feel so strong?
With laughter as a compass, we'll wander afar,
Jellybeans in pockets, best map by far.

So hang up the rucksack, let the dreams unfold,
In the portraits we paint, every mishap is gold.
Celebrate missteps, their stories are sweet,
Just don't eat the map; it's not quite a treat!

The Essence of Wandering Souls

In the dance of socks that mismatched their pairs,
Lies the wisdom of socks—no one really cares.
They frolic and tumble, it's quite a sight,
As they contemplate life over coffee each night.

A coffee cup whispers to a spoon with flair,
Questions of purpose hang thick in the air.
Should I dance in the rain or float on a breeze?
The muffin just nods, 'Do whatever you please.'

Adventures are easy, like pie in a shop,
Mixing odd flavors, with a sprinkle on top.
A cookie winks slyly, 'Sweetness is key,'
Then dives in the milk, as joyful as can be.

So grab your snack friend, and don't take the bait,
For the journey is joy, not a matter of fate.
Each step we forget is a giggle, you see,
In this splendid parade, just be you and me!

Time's Gentle Embrace

Tick, tock, the clock, what a wily old friend,
Teasing our plans as it twists and bends.
A dance with deadlines and late-night snacks,
Oh, the lullabies of procrastination attacks!

The cake in the oven is battling its fate,
While I ponder the wisdom of decorating plate.
Will my flowered icing win the huge prize?
Or just feed the ants with my whimsical lies?

In moments of chaos, we tickle the strain,
As laughter and patience run wild over pain.
So grab a slow dance with that pizza you made,
Share it with time, let the world be delayed.

Savor the seconds like candy that's rare,
For each one you keep is beyond compare.
With a wink and a nod to the great vast unknown,
Let's find joy in the chaos—we're never alone!

The Unraveling of What Was

Once I had a plan, oh so grand,
A list, a chart, with life all planned.
But snacks kept calling, oh what a tease,
I tripped on ambition, fell to my knees.

I bought a cat to help me roam,
He naps on books, claims them as home.
Now I chase him 'round and around,
While my dreams just sit, lost and found.

The things I once wanted, where did they go?
Replaced by cat videos, now that's a show!
Each goal now fits in a teacup small,
As I ponder my fate from the sofa wall.

So here's to plans, all jumbled and torn,
Wrapped up in laughter, a new life is born.
If I can't find my dreams, that's alright,
I'll just lounge 'til they flutter back into sight.

Ghosts of Dreams Half-Remembered

In the night, they linger and sway,
These dreams of mine that went astray.
One danced in a tutu, a remarkable sight,
While another wore socks—oh what a fright!

They whisper sweet nothings, then fade out of view,
Like good pizza toppings, they vanish too.
I reach for a ghost, but he giggles and darts,
Leaving breadcrumbs of wishes, that tug at my heart.

Reality's like a sock with a hole,
Maybe I'll stitch it, or just tend my bowl.
The half-formed visions, they haunt me with cheer,
For ghosts enjoy laughter and snack time right here.

So here's to the dreams that tickle the mind,
May we chase them in laughter, not get too resigned.
For even in chaos, there's joy to be found,
In spectral shenanigans, life spins round!

Ink on the Pages of Time

Once filled with ink, my pages stand,
With doodles and scribbles, a writer's hand.
I meant to pen wisdom, instead wrote a fart,
Now my novel's a joke, a comic art!

Time is a scribbler, with ink all askew,
Crossing out moments, like things that we rue.
Each day a new chapter, with misprints galore,
I laugh at my plot, oh what's in store!

I tried to be serious, a grand literary feat,
But the characters tripped over their own two feet.
My climax? A pie fight, an unplanned event,
With soggy conclusions and laughter well-spent.

So ink flows freely on these pages of mine,
Through mishaps and giggles, my life's a design.
In every mistake, there's a joy that glows bright,
Each written adventure a spark of delight.

Fluttering Pages in the Breeze

I opened a book in the sunshine so bold,
But the pages took flight, oh how they rolled!
Like butterflies dancing, they whirled in delight,
As I chased my ideas into the light.

Each fluttering thought was a quirk on the run,
Some sprouted legs, and others had fun.
I scrambled and leaped, gathering my muse,
With a twist and a turn, we sang a light blues.

The stories once tethered, now skipped through the air,
I laughed and I gasped, as they floated with flair.
In a world that demands serious plight,
I chose to join whimsy, and oh what a sight!

So let the breeze carry my pages with glee,
I'll follow their laughter, and see what will be.
In the dance of the wind, life's joy is revealed,
Fluttering pages, my heart they have healed.

A Symphony of Unsaid Words

Whispers dance in the air,
Like socks lost in the wash.
Dreams collide with a flair,
While we all just blink and squash.

Where did the lunch break go?
Beneath piles of papers and plans.
We sigh and face the flow,
Yet laugh as life pulls us in strands.

The cat's given me advice,
Yet I still trip on the floor.
Should I listen to her muse?
Or just grab a snack and explore?

Words float like balloons released,
Chasing after hopes so grand.
But we're just stuck at the feast,
Waiting for someone to stand.

Guardians of the Never-Was

We wear capes made of regrets,
Fleeting dreams in our pockets.
Wishing to forget the debts,
But popcorn still fills our sockets.

Ghosts of plans dance away,
Pretending they're on the stage.
We smile and hope to play,
While still mulling over the age.

A pizza slice speaks the truth,
Slicing through the mundane drear.
It whispers, "Stay in your youth,"
As we hide behind another beer.

Yet hope lingers like perfume,
Our laughter drowns out the blue.
Together, we face the gloom,
Finding joy in the things we do.

An Ode to Ephemeral Things

Ice cream drips down my hand,
A fleeting moment, oh sweet!
I chase it across the sand,
Laughing as it slides down my seat.

Clouds play tag in the sky,
Just whispers of what's to be.
I watch them float on by,
"Quit giving me all that glee!"

A sock puppet gives a wink,
Oh, how delightful the jest!
We ponder, laugh, and think,
Are we really here, or just guessed?

Every sunrise is a cheer,
Yet I sleep through half the show.
Life's a game, have no fear,
Just sip on that overflow.

The Search for a Celestial Compass

Navigating through the haze,
With coffee grounds as my map.
Count the minutes, count the days,
As I trip and tumble, oh snap!

Stars giggle like old friends,
While I fumble for my keys.
Time, it bends and never ends,
Yet I'm still late, as you see.

A banana peel in my path,
Slips me up, oh what a twist!
Life's math has a funky path,
With answers that often resist.

But I'll keep searching the night,
For beacons that make me grin.
In the chaos, there's delight,
And that's where the fun begins!

The Fabric of Fleeting Winks

In the fabric of dreams we sew,
A button here, a stitch of woe.
Each wink a flash, a fleeting view,
Who knew a nap could feel so new?

With mismatched socks, we dance in pairs,
Spilling coffee, breathing airs.
The world spins on with unkempt grace,
A silly smile on every face.

We chase the clock, but time will taunt,
Its hands are never what they flaunt.
We twirl through chaos, laugh and play,
Unraveling life in a goofy way.

So gather 'round, let's raise a toast,
To silly moments that we love most.
In every wink, a truth appears,
Life's a joke, and so it steers!

Hymns of the Distant Self

In the mirror, a face that grins,
Whispering secrets, wearing sins.
A distant self, both strange and loud,
Reciting hymns to an unseen crowd.

Oh, what a tangled web we weave,
With socks and shoes that rarely cleave.
Each slip and slide, a joyful slip,
Life's a circus on a wild trip.

With every snack that leaves its trace,
We ponder deep at a sloth's pace.
A fleeting thought, a dessert spoon,
Shouting "Eureka!" to the noon.

Let's sing along to our own rhymes,
In the silly dance of borrowed times.
A merry jig, let laughter swell,
For every moment, a private spell.

Alchemy of Everyday Wonders

In the alchemist's lab of the mundane,
We brew up glory, we sip on gain.
A mix of gumdrops, a splash of tears,
Turning chores into comical cheers.

Meet your toaster, a toast with flair,
It sings a tune, a digital air.
Mismatched mugs, they tell a tale,
Of coffee spills and hearty frail.

We juggle dreams like orange balloons,
With confetti hearts and quirky tunes.
A sprinkle of joy, a laugh or two,
In life's grand play, we're the brave few.

So break the mold, let colors clash,
Find the beauty in every splash.
In the mundane's dance, we deeply dive,
With everyday wonders, we come alive!

Lost Treasures in Ordinary Places

In the couch cushions, fortunes lie,
A nickel here, a remote shy.
We sift through crumbs, both lost and found,
The magic in chaos, life unbound.

Underneath the bed, a dust bunny reigns,
Gathering dreams, collecting pains.
A treasure map made of scratched floors,
Leading to laughter behind closed doors.

Ode to the fridge, a cold delight,
Ready to feast, come day or night.
From leftovers dressed in mystery,
To midnight snacks of history.

In mundane spots, where wonders bloom,
We find sweet joys, amidst the gloom.
So cherish the odd, the lost embrace,
In every corner, we find our place!

The Journal of Unseen Wonders

In the quiet hush of night,
My sock drawer holds secrets bright.
A world of lint and missing mates,
Where togs plot schemes and secret dates.

I scribble thoughts in margins wide,
About the socks that choose to hide.
They dance and twirl, what a strange sight,
Chronicles of laundry's endless fight.

Each mat, each thread, has tales to spin,
Of daring socks that won't give in.
Lost the match, but here's the twist,
I find new friends when they persist.

So note this down for future glee,
The mysteries that socks reveal to me.
A pair may hide, a pair may roam,
But in my heart, they'll find a home.

Lost in the Currents of Existence

Waded through a sea of socks,
Only to find I lost my Crocs.
The current pulls, a playful ruse,
I float along with options to choose.

Then a rubber duck came into sight,
Said, "Just relax, it'll be all right!"
I questioned fate and its design,
As toaster crumbs began to whine.

Oh, bubbles burst in soapy cheer,
I ponder deep things while sipping beer.
What makes the duck the king of fun?
When life gives waves, just paddle, run!

Yet here I float, lost but free,
Navigating absurdity with glee.
Life's a splash with all its quirks,
And I'm just laughing, dodging jerks.

The Firefly's Last Flicker

In twilight's glow, the fireflies danced,
A flicker here, a lonely prance.
One brave soul buzzed close to me,
Said, "Don't take life too seriously!"

I watched as he wiggled and swayed,
Claiming the night was never delayed.
His light dimmed low, he sighed and said,
"Shine bright, my friend, before you're dead!"

So I chuckled and gave a cheer,
For every flicker, there's naught to fear.
We'll glow together, under the moon,
Who needs a plan? Just sing a tune!

The briefest of sparks catches my eye,
Laughing at fate as it zooms by.
A short-lived show, but oh, what fun,
Stay bright, stay wild, and never run.

Mapping the Uncharted Heart

With maps in hand, I set my course,
Through chocolate rivers, strange, of course!
X marks the spot, yet I'm just lost,
In the land of crumbs and jam, what a cost!

Each nook unveiled, a new delight,
Tangled in spaghetti, oh what a sight!
My compass spins, but I'm not averse,
To dine on pizza while lost in verse.

So let's pen tales of every bite,
In a world where pizzas are my light.
With doughy dreams, I'll chart and soar,
Mapping the heart, who needs a door?

So here I wander, a quest so sweet,
Finding joy where the flavors meet.
The heart's a puzzle, pick your part,
With every laugh, it's a work of art.

The Hidden Beauty of Everyday

In socks that never match, I dance,
Finding joy in every chance.
A coffee spill becomes a treat,
Life's small wins, oh so sweet.

The cat flips over, strikes a pose,
A nap is where all wisdom grows.
With crumbs upon my favorite chair,
Secret treasures linger there.

The lawn gnome waves, don't take it slow,
He knows the secrets we don't show.
Butterflies gossip, clouds drift by,
In this circus, we all fly high.

In juggling plans that fate denied,
I laugh at dreams that laughed and cried.
Each silly moment, a pearl so bright,
In the chaos, find your light.

Minutes Spent in Longing

I reach for snacks, but there's none left,
Craving chips, I feel quite bereft.
Time ticks by, a slowed parade,
In the pantry, dreams are made.

The clock seems stuck on just one hour,
Anticipation's funny power.
I wonder what the cat might say,
If only time would dance and play.

With each tick, I stir the pot,
Searching for treasures in each thought.
Longing sings a serenade,
When ice cream's gone, plans fade away.

Yet amidst this hunger, I find glee,
In mirages of what's meant to be.
My heart still leaps for snacks once sought,
Life's little cravings, oh what a lot!

When the Silence Speaks

In quiet corners, whispers grew,
An empty room, a ghostly view.
I ponder deep on chocolate cake,
With every fork, oh what's at stake?

The walls may sigh, and curtains sway,
In stillness found, I dance away.
Yet laughter hides within the hush,
In silence, hear the joyful rush.

When words retreat, the giggles bloom,
A sneeze erupts to fill the room.
Each pause a chance for silly pranks,
In silence, life's the best of banks.

So here we sit, as still as toys,
In quiet moments, we find joys.
Life's twinkling stars begin to peek,
In silence, funny things we seek.

The Journey Between Two Heartbeats

Between each thump, a world unfolds,
Strange tales of laughter yet untold.
A leap, a bob, we float and sway,
Life's every heartbeat finds its play.

With every pause, a snack we dare,
Breadsticks stand like soldiers there.
Heartbeat races for the fun,
In this dance, we've just begun.

Tick-tock, tick-tock, let's not rush,
The chaos turns to joyful hush.
In every beat, a chance to trip,
On googly eyes or a cupcake sip.

So take this journey, jump and shout,
Live in the moments, cast out doubt.
From beat to beat, we'll laugh, we'll sigh,
In this grand ride, oh me, oh my!

The Remains of Unlived Lives

In corners, dust bunnies dance with glee,
While coffee mugs hold a history.
To-do lists mock me with their sly grin,
Forgotten dreams wrapped in a din.

I ponder choices, oh what a jest,
Should I've chosen jelly or the zest?
Regrets pile high, like laundry amassed,
As I chuckle at the tales that won't last.

The days tick by with a wink and a nudge,
While my aspirations politely fudge.
Plans skitter like cats in the night,
As I laugh at the things I don't write.

Yet here I stand, with a grin on my face,
A jester in this chaotic race.
Embracing the mess, the joy, the absurd,
In lives unlived, sweet mischiefs stirred.

Lanterns in the Maze of Thoughts

Wandering through a labyrinth bright,
With lanterns flickering, just out of sight.
I trip on ideas, oh what a sight,
While squirrels debate if to take flight.

Mismatched socks toss in the breeze,
They chuckle at my worries with ease.
Lightbulbs pop like popcorn in my head,
As squirrels compare where dreams are led.

The walls echo with laughter and noise,
As I chase after whims like lost toys.
Thoughts zigzag, dance, and collide,
Turning wisdom into a cheeky ride.

I drift in this maze, feeling so bold,
Among echoes of stories waiting to be told.
Finding humor in twists and in turns,
In this tangled journey, joy always burns.

Beyond the Shadows of Certainty

Certainty left on a train that won't stop,
As doubts play baseball, fielding the flop.
I toss my plans into the air,
Like confetti dreams without a care.

Questions swirl like leaves in the wind,
Each twist and turn leaves me quite pinned.
Balloons of hope bob, bickering bright,
Over who gets to reign in the twilight.

Jokes slip through like shadows at noon,
As I wrestle with the world's funny tune.
Of all the answers I've tripped over,
Many were just the punchline of a lover.

Yet through the riddle, laughter breaks free,
As I unearth the lightness in me.
In places unknown, where jesters roam,
I find a new path to call my home.

The Alchemy of Dust and Dreams

In the attic, where dreams lie in wait,
Dust bunnies conspire to seal my fate.
I weigh my regrets like feathers and stones,
While echoes of laughter fill the bones.

Mismatched ideas, potions in line,
Brewing a whimsy that tastes like wine.
I mix up my thoughts with a spoonful of grace,
While giggles of wisdom dance in the space.

Turning old schemes into sparkling new,
I tickle the past till it blooms in the dew.
Jokes float like bubbles up to the sky,
As I wonder what else I can defy.

Here in this chaos, magic takes flight,
Crafting tales that make me delight.
In the alchemy of laughter and sighs,
I find treasures where my heart lies.

Chasing Shadows and Starlight

In a world of fleeting rays,
We trip on our own shoelaces,
Trying to grasp the night's soft glow,
But end up chatting with a crow.

The stars wink down from high above,
While shadows tease like a lost glove,
We dance in circles, spin around,
Tripping over truths we've never found.

We scribble notes on paper boats,
And wonder if they float or gloat,
In puddles formed by dreams and sighs,
Where laughter hides behind goodbyes.

So here we are, in cosmic jest,
Finding joy in the quirkiest quest,
With every step, a story starts,
In the silly maze of our own hearts.

The Melody of the Unsaid

Whispers bloom in the noise of life,
Like strawberries growing in strife,
We dance around what should be clear,
Sending giggles to the distant ear.

In a tune that hums through the air,
We sing of woes and dreams laid bare,
Not every note is meant to shine,
Some slip through cracks like forgotten wine.

Silly secrets ride on the breeze,
Hiding behind the giggles and squeals,
In every chuckle, we find a rhyme,
That bends and twists, mocking time.

So let's embrace the unsaid song,
Where laughter reigns, we all belong,
With every chuckle, we set it free,
A melody, a joke, just you and me.

Navigating the Currents of Thought

Thoughts are ships adrift at sea,
Sailing on waves of irony,
We map the stars with a shattered pen,
And ponder if they'll guide us again.

In whirlpools of worry, we often dive,
Chasing each thought that comes alive,
Dodging the storms of regret and fear,
While ice cream dreams often reappear.

A compass spins, confused in hand,
Pointing to snacks instead of land,
As we navigate these silly tides,
With laughter, our trusty guide abides.

So let's cast off, let worries unwind,
Sail on the silliness, embracing the blind,
For in these waters of thoughts unfurled,
We find the fun in this wacky world.

Diary Pages Past, Future Unwritten

Diary pages fold and curl,
Like secret dreams that swirl,
Each entry whispers tales of yore,
Of socks misplaced and an open door.

Crayon colors splash with glee,
Recording moments just for me,
As typos dance in bashful rows,
Highlighting life's delightful woes.

The future waits, a blank white space,
With doodles ready to embrace,
But today we giggle, laugh, and sing,
Over silly things and random bling.

So flip those pages, set thoughts free,
Write what tickles, what makes you squeal,
In every line, let laughter bloom,
For even chaos has its room.

Future Unwritten

An empty page lies in the dawn,
Where dreams and giggles are softly drawn,
We scribble wishes with wobbly lines,
Hoping for fortune, and maybe some signs.

Where paths diverge like forks in the pie,
We'll taste each slice, oh me, oh my,
With flavors both silly and a bit bizarre,
Eating our way to the next bizarre star.

Tick-tock goes the clock of jest,
While we draft our plans, a silly quest,
A treasure map without much treasure,
Filled with laughter, our greatest treasure.

So pen your future, let it unwind,
With joyful chaos filled with the blind,
For even uncertain letters can cheer,
When you write with giggles, year after year.

Moments Tucked in the Spaces

On Tuesday I misplaced my sock,
In a drawer where it might just walk.
A kitchen full of half-done meals,
Makes me wonder what 'adult' feels.

The cat sits judging from the chair,
With eyes that say, "Do you even care?"
I aim for bliss in tiny bits,
Yet find joy in even odder fits.

Lost my keys, they're in plain sight,
I shout, "Why's this not alright?"
With coffee cups as my companions,
We navigate this game of ran-ions.

Yet laughter rings amidst the chaos,
Like finding treasure in the gloss.
We dance with life's absurd parade,
In a world where worry does degrade.

Puzzles of Time's Tattered Quilt

Threads of chaos stitch my day,
Unraveling in a funny way.
I tripped on thoughts from long before,
And laughed at dreams, strange and sore.

Yesterday's wisdom feels so tough,
Like diets made of pizza fluff.
I ponder where my marbles went,
While sandwich crumbs are my best friend.

The clock ticks on with no respect,
It mocks my time and intellect.
Yet in this madcap rush we gamble,
To find delight in every ramble.

So here's to life, a quirky game,
Where laughter is the ultimate aim.
I'll wear mismatched socks with pride,
For in this mess, my joy will hide.

Tender Echoes Beneath the Noise

In the noise, I found a song,
Where giggles and chaos both belong.
Whispers wrapped in silly hats,
The universe delights in spats.

Moments slip like butter on toast,
And the fridge hums, weirdly boast.
I lost my thoughts; they're out on break,
But they send postcards for goodness' sake.

Inside my head, a circus thrives,
With juggling dreams and clumsy jives.
A parade of hopes that come and go,
Tickling me in this bright show.

So I'll celebrate this kite of cheer,
Where every tumble leads to near.
In echoes low beneath the buzz,
I find the joy in happy fuzz.

Where the Unseen Becomes Known

Where shadows dance and light plays tricks,
I stumble over my own quick fix.
A grocery list? It's quite a laugh,
I left it home on my other half.

The cat swipes at invisible foes,
While I misplace my mental clothes.
This circus of mishaps feels so real,
That I stop to giggle and spin the wheel.

A bite of pie, oh sweet delight,
As I ponder through this nonsensical flight.
The mundane sings a quirky tune,
Beneath the stars and lazy moon.

I'll toast to journeys, big and small,
In this bizarre carnival called it all.
For every stumble leads us to find,
The humor swaying, beautifully blind.

Roots of a Story Untold

In the garden of forgetters, we plant our seeds,
Watering dreams with our daily misdeeds.
Plucking at notions, strange and bizarre,
Finding confessions in a candy jar.

The cactus of wisdom pokes at our mind,
While the daisies of doubt are ever so kind.
Each petal a giggle, each thorn a surprise,
A patchwork of laughter, where truth often lies.

We dig up the tales buried deep in the yard,
Playing at archaeologists, it isn't too hard.
With shovels of humor and buckets of cheer,
We unearth the past with a tickle and sneer.

So let's dance with our stories, both wild and untamed,
Collecting the moments, forever unnamed.
With roots intertwined in a whimsical dance,
We chuckle at life as we take our chance.

Beneath the Surface: Truths Hidden

Under the pool of the ordinary, we splash,
Divin' for truths, making quite the crash.
With goggles of giggles, we peek through the haze,
Finding our laughter in the murky maze.

The goldfish of wisdom swims round and round,
While ducks of distraction make silly sounds.
We slip on intentions, both slippery and sweet,
In the carnival waters, life's never discreet.

So we paddle through nonsense, ancient and wise,
Unraveling riddles disguised as good pies.
With straws made of memory, we sip on delight,
Mixing up stories like a bee in its flight.

In the whirlpool of chaos, we hang on tight,
Surfing through nonsense beneath the moonlight.
Every splash a reminder, every ripple a jest,
Let's celebrate nonsense—it's truly the best!

The Unsung Chorus of Our Days

A symphony's brewing in the chaos we chase,
With maracas of memories, we keep up the pace.
Dancing on calendars, twirling through time,
Singing off-key in a rhythmless rhyme.

Heralded by laughter, the chorus takes flight,
Providing the score to our day and our night.
The tambourine's jingles ring out as we spin,
While the silent shofar calls us all in.

Each verse is a mishap, each note a delight,
With harmonies tangled, our hearts feel so light.
We juggle our sanity while on pogo sticks,
Dancing bare-footed, trading decorative tricks.

So let's join the orchestra, make some rare noise,
With spatulas, banjos, and imaginary toys.
In the concert of living, we find our own way,
Celebrating chaos in the unsung parade.

When Memories Become Shadows

Shadows on sidewalks, they dance and they prance,
Taking us back to that fateful first glance.
Like ghosts in the attic, they whisper and tease,
A game of charades that no one can freeze.

With every footstep, they flit out of sight,
Chasing the echoes of our silly plight.
The shadow of lunch breaks, the shade of a date,
Each fleeting impression becomes second-rate.

Caught in the glow of nostalgia so sweet,
We reminisce moments when life was a treat.
With layers of laughter, we peel back the skin,
Finding the joy in the mess we've been in.

When the shadows retreat, as all shadows do,
We'll wave goodbye, with the fondness we knew.
In the twilight of memories, they linger and sway,
A collage of laughter from yesterday.

The Veil of Ordinary Days

Each morning's coffee, a potion brewed,
A dance with socks, mismatched and skewed.
The clock alarm yells, but I snooze and sigh,
Waking up late, as dreams wave goodbye.

To-do lists grow like weeds in my mind,
Yet Netflix whispers, so sweet and unkind.
I ponder my plans while I munch on a snack,
And wonder if gazing at walls counts as 'back'.

Laundry piles up like a mountain of dread,
I'd fold it right now, but there's cheese I must spread.
Days slip away, like ice on a lake,
Perhaps I'll do something, or maybe I'll bake.

So here's to the hours that slip through our fingers,
To laughter and chaos that endlessly lingers.
In this grand little circus, we juggle and play,
Finding joy in the mess of our ordinary day.

A Treasure Map of Fleeting Days

I searched for treasure on a day oh so bright,
A map made of crumbs, led me left, then right.
With X marking spots for naps and for snacks,
Adventuring bravely through fridge's high stacks.

I found a gold coin, a chocolate surprise,
From the bottom of bags, it's candy that lies.
X marks the chill, where ice cream's stored tight,
The true pirate's prize on a lazy night.

Navigating life with a fork in my hand,
Exploring the depths of my junk food land.
Each bite a compass, each slurp a clue,
It's a map of delight, no treasure's more true.

So here's to the adventure, let us raise our spoons,
To spoiling dinner with chocolate-filled tunes.
A treasure well-hidden, a joy to behold,
In the ordinary chaos, let each day unfold.

Threads of Connection in the Void

In the land of the lost, I hunt for my keys,
Each room a black hole, with odd shaped decrees.
I chat with my plants, they seem to agree,
That loneliness echoes, like a lost bumblebee.

I message my friends, but they often don't write,
Perhaps they're lost too, like socks in the night.
A virtual hug, through screens we all crave,
Existence made sweeter, with memes that we save.

In the void, I find wisdom, or maybe it's snacks,
A sandwich of thoughts, with laughter on cracks.
Though life's thread unravels, with humor I weave,
Tangled connections, but we never leave.

So let's share our stories, these symphonies odd,
A chorus of madness, where laughter's the nod.
In this tangled up web, we twirl and we twist,
Finding joy in the chaos, in moments we've missed.

A Garden of Forgotten Intentions

In the garden of dreams, where daffodils laugh,
We plant silly worries, then cut them in half.
The carrots of thought sprout under big skies,
While daisies remind us to don't take the highs.

A weed named 'Perhaps' creeps into my plot,
I prune it with reason, plot twist, it's caught!
"Oh what could have been," says the garden gnome,
While taking a break from his typical roam.

Sunshine and rainbows hold strong their decree,
That life's just a garden of chuckles, you see?
We water our hopes with laughter's good cheer,
And pull up each sorrow, 'cause joy's always near.

So gather the blooms of your whims as they shine,
In the garden of intentions that's whimsically mine.
With roots intertwined, let us giggle and sway,
In this magical place where we frolic all day.

Echoes in the Absence of Purpose

In a world where socks go to hide,
The left goes left, the right feels pride.
A quest for keys, an endless race,
Is my couch a portal to another space?

The cat thinks it's grand, a true philosopher,
While I'm stuck here, a procrastinator.
Sipping coffee, I ponder the day,
Will my plants finally learn how to sway?

Neighbors shout loudly, but no one hears,
They argue with echoes, not shedding tears.
Life's little riddles make me laugh and cringe,
Next time I'll put the milk in the fridge!

When pots and pans dance in the night,
Perhaps they're trying to get it right.
In the chaos of crumbs and spilled drinks,
Who knew wisdom could come from the clinks?

Threads of Existence Unraveled

Knitting my fate with yarn from a cat,
Each stitch I tug reveals my life's chat.
The pattern's a mess, a vibrant display,
Who knew the universe loved to play?

Life's a puzzle, pieces that don't fit,
I swear I had a plan; oh, where did I sit?
With crumbs for inspiration, I sketch my plan,
What's next? A dance-off with a biscuit can?

The to-do list grows, like weeds in my mind,
I chase down the rainbow, but it's hard to find.
My coffee goes cold as I question it all,
Like balancing books at a carnival stall.

With mismatched socks and a loaf shaped like art,
I wear my confusion like a badge of smart.
Threads of existence tangled in a twirl,
Celebrate chaos, give life a whirl!

When Shadows Seek the Light

Shadows stroll in with a tip of their hats,
They giggle and whisper, play tricks like cats.
I shine a light, but they dance out of sight,
Fickle as fortune in the middle of night.

One tried to borrow my sense of direction,
He left with my keys; what a strange collection!
I chased him around with a broom in my hand,
Turns out he was lost in a world oh-so-grand.

Sunshine arrives with a bright, cheeky smile,
Says 'Join the parade, let's walk a while!'
We laugh at the mishaps, the wild, silly blight,
And shadows retreat, too embarrassed to fight.

So here's to the flickers that come and that go,
In this dance of existence, we're all in the show.
When shadows are silly, just take them in stride,
Life's more like laughter than the things we abide.

The Atlas of Lost Dreams

Once I had dreams, now they're like socks,
Hidden in nooks, just a mix of odd clocks.
Mapping out paths in a curious maze,
Each turn brings humor, a reason to gaze.

The atlas was drawn with crayons of glee,
With smudges and doodles—a masterpiece, see?
Holding my hopes like a balloon in a breeze,
It drifts and it wobbles, yet still aims to tease.

In a world full of maps that get lost in the fold,
I scribble my laughter, daring and bold.
With pancakes for breakfast and socks that don't match,
I surrender my worries to the sweet morning batch.

So here's to the journeys we stumble and chase,
Our atlas of dreams has a comical grace.
With each little giggle, we scratch out the seams,
Find joy in the chaos, it's more than it seems.

The Color of Unanswered Whys

Why's the sky so blue today?
I forgot my shades, so hey!
Elves stealing socks in the night,
Dance in chaos, what a sight!

A pigeon with a tilted hat,
Says he knows where next I'm at.
Juggling thoughts I can't control,
Finding laughter is my goal!

The toaster's got its toast on hold,
My coffee's brewed but never bold.
Dreams are like the socks I lose,
Maybe they're wearing fancy shoes.

So here I stand with silly plans,
Making wishes with my hands.
What's the secret? I can't see,
But maybe it's just being me!

Navigating the Labyrinth of Now

In the maze of mundane grins,
I trip on thoughts and loss of spins.
A rubber duck leads, quacking loud,
While I pretend to be proud.

Google Maps can't find a way,
To this tangle of my day.
Do we all just sort of guess?
Waltzing through this lovely mess?

Cats in windows plotting schemes,
As I ponder life and dreams.
Onward, forward, losing track,
Shall I return? No turning back!

So I'll laugh at what I've found,
In this riddle wrapped around.
Numbers, words, absurdity—
Navigating happily!

Crumpled Pages in the Book of Time

Once I wrote a letter, see?
But I spilled tea — a tragedy!
Time's just a sneaky little thief,
Taking moments like a chief.

Crumpled corners tell the tales,
Of missed trains and wandering gales.
Under the bed? An old pizza slice,
Seems nostalgia comes with its price.

Tick-tock clocks with sticky hands,
Guide me on these silly lands.
I scribble notes on napkins stained,
Hope the wisdom's not all drained!

But every line I twist and fold,
Makes life's canvas bright and bold.
So here's to pages, torn yet fine,
In this book, I'll sip some wine!

Reflections in an Empty Teacup

Peering in my teacup small,
Where's my fortune? I hear a call!
Swirling leaves and steam arise,
Telling tales of greatest whys.

An empty cup, a single thought,
Where's the answer that I sought?
Perhaps it's hiding with the cream,
Or snoozing deep in scone-filled dreams.

Kettles whistle sweet delight,
Should I ponder or take flight?
The cat looks wise, it knows the score,
Did I forget what's at the core?

So I sip the air, taste the void,
In this moment, simply enjoyed.
Life's a brew of bitter, sweet,
And emptiness can feel complete!

The Art of Silent Conversations

In crowded rooms we speak with eyes,
A nod, a wink, a sly disguise.
Words may fail, yet smiles can shine,
Silent chats, a crafty line.

We trade our thoughts through quiet grins,
In awkward pauses, true chat begins.
A shrug, a laugh, a shared bite,
Who needs a voice when moods feel right?

Lost in chatter of daily grind,
Our minds drift off, but hearts rewind.
A silent dance we twirl along,
Communicating feels so wrong!

So raise a glass to silence loud,
In unspoken fun, we feel so proud.
For when the world gets way too chatty,
Let's celebrate our current natty!

Footprints on the Sand of Time

Each footprint left upon the shore,
Is evidence we were once more.
Little dips and doodles we make,
A shoeless dance, a chance to shake.

The tide rolls in to claim its prize,
Our footprints washed, to our surprise.
Yet in the sand, our giggles stay,
Buried treasures of yesterday.

What's left behind is not just grain,
It tells of joy and silly rain.
Each step a sign of fun unfurled,
Though tides may wash away our world.

So let us leap and strut and sing,
In every print, joy's what we bring.
The sand may fade but laugh remains,
In goofy tales and silly gains!

Beneath the Surface of Ordinary

In daily drudges and tiresome tasks,
Lies a world where whimsy basks.
Beneath the dull and mundane sheen,
Are hidden laughs, if you glean.

The coffee spills, the toast may burn,
Yet laughter's reign is what we yearn.
Life's simple quirks, oh what a tease,
In mishaps, we discover ease.

Routine's a trickster, playing coy,
It steals our peace but gives us joy.
What seems so plain might start to gleam,
When we embrace the chaos theme.

So peek beneath that vacant stare,
And find the giggles hiding there.
For mundane whispers secrets bright,
Turn frowns to laughter, day to night!

Echoes of Unspoken Wishes

In quiet corners where dreams conspire,
Whispers echo of desires higher.
No words can spill, but thoughts can dance,
In the space where chances prance.

The wish to fly, to eat dessert,
To tell a joke or wear a skirt.
We smile and nod but never dare,
To voice the hopes floating in the air.

Yet in those dreams where giggles form,
Are echoes loud that take the norm.
Unspoken wishes, like bubbles burst,
In realms of fun, we've quenched our thirst.

So here's to wishes left unvoiced,
An inner child that still rejoiced.
For in the silence lies the cheer,
A rhyme of life we hold so dear!

The Quest for Clarity

In a world that spins and twirls,
A quest for truth, oh how it swirls.
I search for answers, not much luck,
Just a sock, and a stubborn duck.

Where are the guides with wisdom bright?
I find more sense in pizza night.
Questions dance like silly sprites,
While I just chase my lost delights.

Maps are drawn on napkins stained,
Paths confuse, and minds are drained.
Yet laughter bubbles, warms the heart,
In this delightful, twisted art.

In puzzles wrapped in facts and fun,
I laugh and frolic, come undone.
For every clue that leads me astray,
I find a chuckle lights the way.

The Light Behind Closed Doors

Behind each door, a secret dwells,
Like socks with holes, or hidden wells.
I pry them open, take a peek,
What's there? A cat that sneezes geek!

A lamp that just won't light the night,
And dreams that flutter out of sight.
I laugh at whispers, shadows, calls,
For wisdom hides behind these walls.

I set my sights on silly things,
Like dancing weed and tinfoil wings.
What's a life without absurd?
Just a boring, silent word.

So close the door, but not too tight,
Let giggles in, let in the light.
For every glance inside reveals,
Life's a circus, full of squeals.

The Universe Inside a Grain of Sand

A grain of sand, so small and meek,
Yet holds the tales that seas do speak.
I ponder deep on this small find,
And wonder if it's lost my mind.

The beach is vast, a world of spree,
But here's a universe for me.
With tiny friends, I build a throne,
Out of the moments that I own.

Eons captured in its weight,
And just as old as my dinner plate.
Each speck contains stardust dreams,
Bound together with cosmic beams.

So when in doubt, just take a scoop,
Life's grand ideas fit in this loop.
A mirage, a giggle, a sandy dance,
Here lies the fun, in fate's odd chance.

Secrets Held by Time

Oh time, you crafty, pesky friend,
With all your turns and twists, we bend.
You hide behind clocks, with ticking flair,
And keep us laughing, pulling hair.

In dusty books, old jokes reside,
Along with dreams we tried to hide.
Tick-a-tock, the minutes tease,
As we juggle errands and a sneeze.

What secrets lie in your embrace?
A dance, a stumble, a silly face?
Oh, to unravel your sly riddle,
I'd wear a hat, or play the fiddle.

So let's toast to you, oh time so sly,
With snacks and giggles, let's not be shy.
For every moment's a cheeky jest,
In this merry game, we're truly blessed.

The Serenity of Still Moments

In a world of constant hurry,
The lost socks hold a story.
Time to put the coffee down,
And wear that silly crown.

The cat judges from the chair,
As I trip over thin air.
Days float by like fluffy clouds,
While I'm lost in laughing crowds.

Every pause is a quirky dance,
In pajama pants, I take a chance.
Moments freeze, collecting dust,
In chaos, we learn to trust.

Bubble tea and wobbly road,
Encourage hearts to share their load.
With every sip, a giggle or two,
Life's hilarity shines right through.

The Heartbeat Underneath

Beneath the chaos, a rhythm plays,
It's like a tune that oddly sways.
Dancing chickens cross the street,
With two left feet, they can't be beat.

Life's a ride on wobbly wheels,
A cupcake truck that always steals.
In random moments, joy appears,
With goofy wigs and frothy beers.

Laughter bubbles, floating high,
Like a kite stuck in the sky.
Jokes line up like cars at dusk,
In silly socks, we find our trust.

Heartbeat thumping, quite absurd,
As the world spins—a merry bird.
Underneath it all, we jest,
With goofy grins, we're truly blessed.

Bridges of Introspection

Over bridges made of dreams,
We chat with puddles, or so it seems.
Pondering life, as we munch on fries,
Listening close to ducky sighs.

Reflections bounce like rubber balls,
In mirrors shaped like funky walls.
What's the rush? Let's take a break,
And chat with frogs by the lake.

Naps are bridges to the curious,
As we ponder what's mysterious.
Float on thoughts like boats on streams,
In giggling fits, we create our dreams.

Cozy corners hold our thoughts,
In crumpled socks, our laughter's caught.
Build a bridge with laughter's grace,
Through silly times, we find our place.

Whispers of a Forgotten Dawn

At dawn, when sleepy heads arise,
The toast pops up with gremlin size.
Whispers of yesterday's dreams,
In a world that giggles and gleams.

The sleepy sun peeks through the trees,
Tickled pink by the morning breeze.
A bird's serenade of clucks and coos,
Plays hide-and-seek with all the blues.

Each coffee sip, a lingering jest,
While cereal dances, trying its best.
We forget the woes, embrace the fun,
Underneath the lazy sun.

So, let the dawn drape us in grace,
As we tumble through this happy space.
With all the giggles that we've seen,
Life's sweet is but a whimsical dream.

9 781805 661412